The Rabbit Dance

An Iroquois Tale • Retold by Avelyn Davidson
Illustrated by Xiangyi Mo and Jingwen Wang

Long, long ago, some hunters were looking for food. They crept quietly through the forest, hoping to find some animals.

Suddenly, one of the hunters lifted his bow. The hunters all stopped. They stared in amazement.

In a clearing in the forest, the hunters saw the largest rabbit they had ever seen. It was huge. It was as large as a small bear.

"That rabbit will feed the people of our village for a week," one of the hunters whispered.

As the hunters took aim, the enormous rabbit lifted its head. It looked at the hunters. It did not run away. Instead, it lifted one of its feet and thumped on the ground.

Suddenly, rabbits appeared from all directions. They ran to the huge rabbit. They didn't look at the hunters.

The big rabbit stamped its foot. It sounded like a drumbeat. The little rabbits made a circle around the big rabbit and began to dance.

The rabbits danced on their own. They danced together. Around and around they went, in time to the beat of the big rabbit's foot.

Soon the hunters found themselves tapping their feet to the beat, too. They found themselves swaying to the rhythm.

Suddenly, the big rabbit stopped thumping the ground. It jumped high in the air. It jumped right over the hunters' heads and disappeared.

The little rabbits all took off in different directions. Soon the clearing was empty.

The hunters were amazed.

"That must have been the chief of the rabbits," said the leader of the hunters. "We must go back to the village and ask our clan mother what this means."

When the hunters got back to the village, they told everyone what they had seen.

The clan mother listened carefully to their tale. She was very wise and knew about the ways of the animals.

When the hunters had finished their tale, the clan mother handed their leader a drum.

"Play the rhythm that the rabbit chief played," she said.

The leader of the hunters played the beat on the drum. Soon all the villagers were tapping their feet and swaying to the rhythm.

"That is a very good rhythm," said the clan mother. "Now show me the dance that the rabbits danced."

The hunters made a circle around their leader. The leader played the beat and the hunters began to dance.

First, they danced by themselves.
Then they danced together.
Around and around they went,
to the beat of the leader's drum.

When the dance was over, the clan mother smiled.

"I know what this means," she said. "The rabbits know that we hunt them for food. They know that we wear their skins. They know how important they are to us. The rabbit chief has shown us a special dance. We must do the dance to thank the rabbits for all the things they give to our people."

The leader picked up the drum. He began to play the beat that the rabbit chief had played. The villagers made a big circle. They swayed to the beat. They tapped their feet to the rhythm.

They danced on their own. They danced together. Around and around they went, to the beat of the leader's drum.

So a new dance was learned by the villagers. To this day, the Iroquois people do the dance to thank the rabbits for everything they give them.